The Prince and the Pauper

MUSIC BY NEIL BERG

LYRICS BY NEIL BERG AND BERNIE GARZIA

*Omitted from the New York production

Original cast recording released on Jay Records

ISBN 0-634-08679-0

7777 W. BLUEMOUND RD. P.O. BOX 13819 MILWAUKEE, WI 53213

In Australia Contact:
Hal Leonard Australia Pty. Ltd.
4 Lentara Court
Cheltenham, Victoria, 3192 Australia
Email: ausadmin@halleonard.com

Visit Hal Leonard Online at
www.halleonard.com

THRILL OF ADVENTURE

Music by NEIL BERG
Lyric by NEIL BERG and BERNIE GARZIA

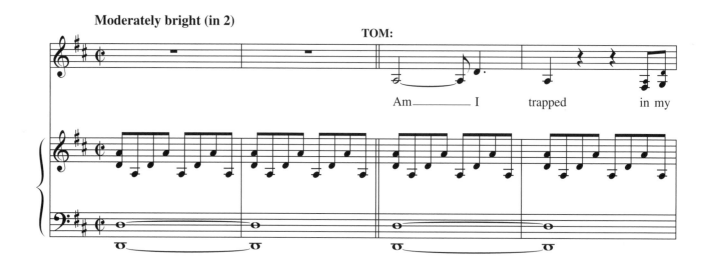

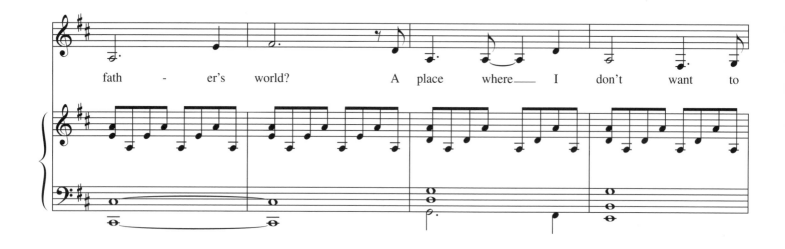

close my eyes and wake up no - bil - i -

With energy

ty   I've got this feel-ing in - side—— me   It's filled with

mag - ic and my - st'ry   Oh, some - one please tell—— me   what can—— it

be   There is a voice that is cry - ing: Go out and

live, yes, live! Can that voice be

me? I'd be the Prince of Eng - land

dressed in royal at - tire "You can call me, 'Sire'

Please, get off the floor..." I'd dance in lav - ish

ball-rooms robed in gowns of gold What a sight to be -

hold, Could life be an-y-thing more?

Maestoso

PRINCE:

I am the Prince of

Eng-land I have ab-so-lute power Ser-vants run and cower

Poco accel.

Poco più mosso

THE KING OF OFFAL COURT

Music by NEIL BERG
Lyric by NEIL BERG and BERNIE GARZIA

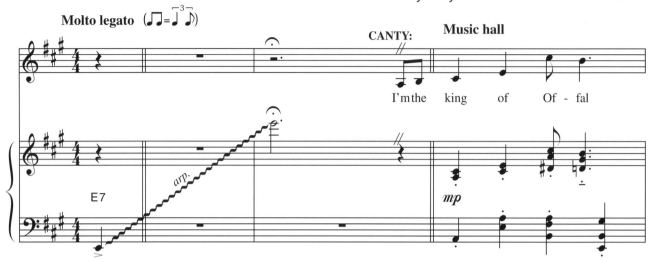

(swing 8ths)

sport And I al-ways help my peo-ple out of

Poco rit.
(straight 8ths)

ev - 'ry piece of jew-elry that they tout a-bout And if I'm in a lurch, hell, I'll

A tempo

ev - en rob the church to prove I'm e - qual - ly de-vout So

Rubato

boy don't think I'm be-ing hard on you I'm just do-ing what ev - 'ry good

ALMOST HOME

Music by NEIL BERG
Lyric by NEIL BERG and BERNIE GARZIA

Slow and majestic (colla voce)

MILES:

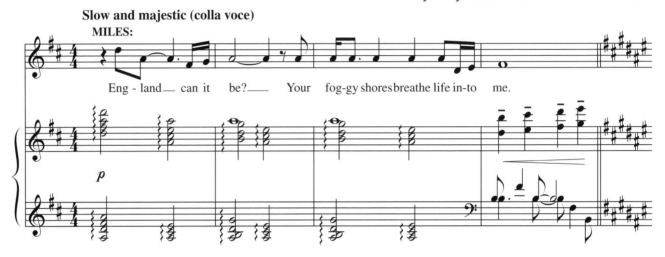

Eng - land— can it be?— Your fog-gy shores breathe life in-to me.

p

Molto rit.

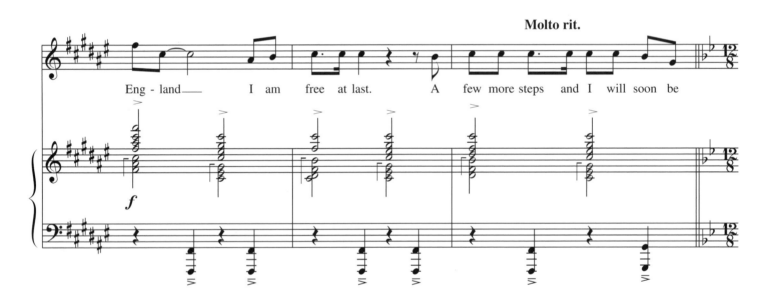

Eng - land— I am free at last. A few more steps and I will soon be

f

Swashbuckling (not too fast)

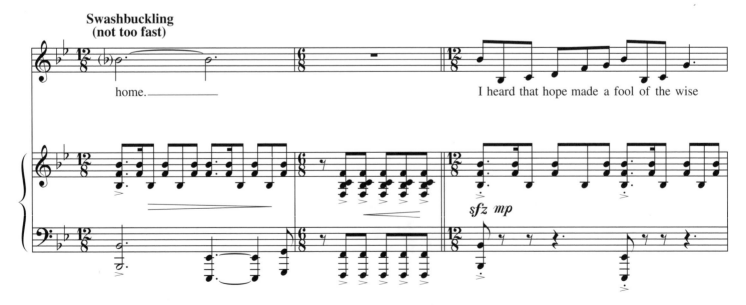

home.— I heard that hope made a fool of the wise

sfz mp

Wound-ed the heart and it blind-ed the eyes Yet hope was my ha-ven, and home is my prize And

here I am!_____ Damn all the time I spent locked in a cell I

may not see heav-en,____ but swear I've seen hell! Es-caped with my looks... and a sto-ry to tell And

here I am!_____ Al-most home___ A boy left, but a man re-turns

Al - most home Re-fus-ing to die!_____ A few more steps to

jour - ney's end_____ I'm al - most

home_____ Fa-ther will cry like a lass on the brink

Hugh will raise glass af - ter glass and we'll drink! And Ed-ith I'll ra-vage, or bet-ter, I think

gent - ly kiss her hand   Al - most home_____ An

an - swered prayer, to touch her hair   Al - most home   Dry-ing her

sub. **mp**   **p** *dolce*   *cresc.*

eyes_____ With love - ly Ed - ith as my

mf

A bit slower

bride_____ I'm al - most home.

p

A bit brighter

love - ly Ed - ith as my bride_____ For

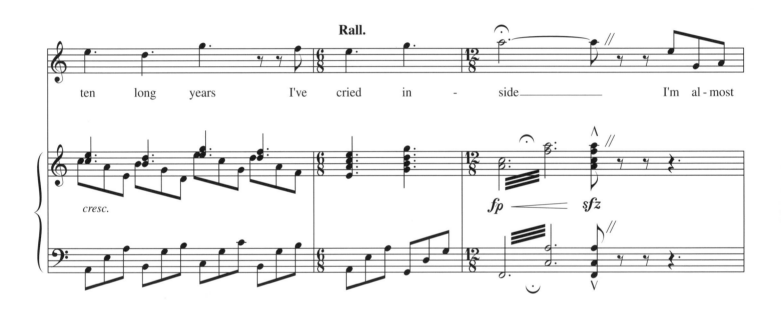

ten long years I've cried in - side_____ I'm al - most

A tempo

home Home!_____

LONELY

Music and Lyrics by
NEIL BERG

Moderato in 4

EDITH:

How did you sur - vive? Is your love a-

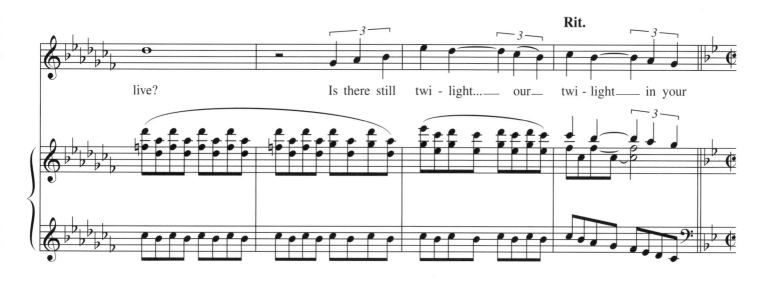

live? Is there still twi - light... our twi - light in your

Slower in 2

eyes?

Ev-'ry-where I hear you____ Ev-'ry place I see you____

Ev-'ry-day I say, "My God, please be the one." But

ev-'ry-time he turns to go, I know you're gone

Still I car - ry on with-out____ you.

Rit.   **Più mosso**

Lone-ly is the way I feel with-out you.

Lone-ly is the way I feel with-out you

Più mosso
MILES:

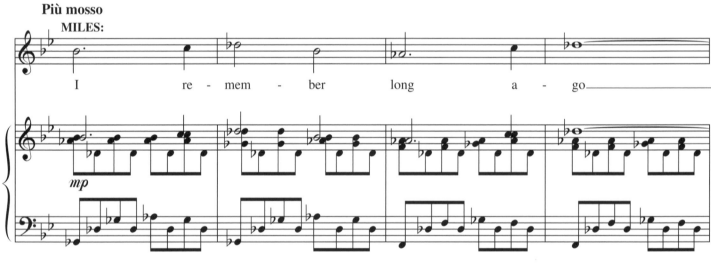

I re-mem - ber long a - go

_mp_

A night like this

EDITH:
You once proved to me that love was real

EDITH:
Sealed with twi-light's sec-ret kiss...

MILES:
Sealed with twi-light's sec-ret kiss...

Rit.

Più mosso

Moderate 2

MILES:
Ev-'ry-where I hear you

EDITH:

Ev-'ry-where I hear you____ Ev-'ry place I see you____

Ev-'ry place I see you____

My God, please be the

Ev-'ry day I say, "My God, please be the

one Still ev-'ry-day I need you here

one."

Ev-'ry day I'm lone - ly

sub. *mp* *cresc. poco a poco*

IF I WERE YOU

Music by NEIL BERG
Lyric by NEIL BERG and BERNIE GARZIA

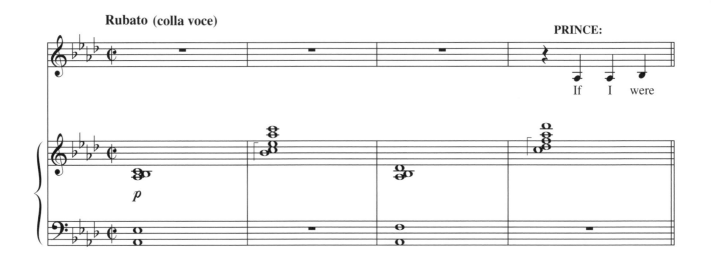

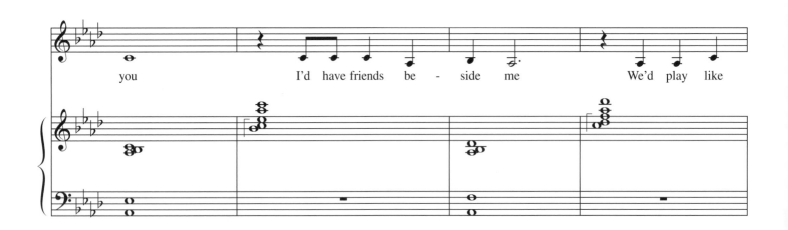

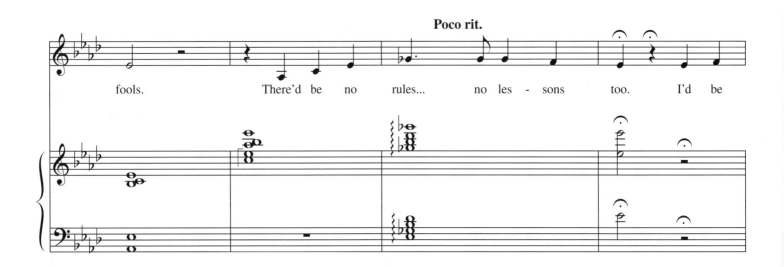

seems_____ we're on - ly dream - ing 'Cause

A tempo

you don't know you've got it good, but boy, I think you should.___ 'Cause

that's what I would do if I were...

...if I were you!___

IS THIS LOVE?

Music by NEIL BERG
Lyric by NEIL BERG and BERNIE GARZIA

LADY JANE:

It's the laugh in his smile It's the smile in his laugh As he

of-fers a bis-cuit and spits on my half And he shouts when I sing And he

shouts when I pray And he should-n't be shout-ing I guess that's just his

mem-ber_____ the em - ber_____ 'til you

sub. *p*   < *mp*   <

cresc. poco a poco

(LADY JANE:) "But I don't understand!"

die!_____ Is this

p   cresc. poco a poco   *sfz*

love?_____ I'm con - tent with my life   Love...____ I'm a du - ti - ful wife

f

LADY JANE:

Love..._____ Af - ter so man - y years Af - ter so man - y tears... La - dy,

mp   cresc.

ache_____ Is this

EDITH: LADY EDITH: BOTH:

JANE:

love?_____ I'm a - fraid that it's so   Love..._____ When you   can-not let go

Love..._____ When the   an - swer you knows's in the   ques - tion you

Più mosso

SIMPLE BOY

Music by NEIL BERG
Lyric by NEIL BERG and BERNIE GARZIA

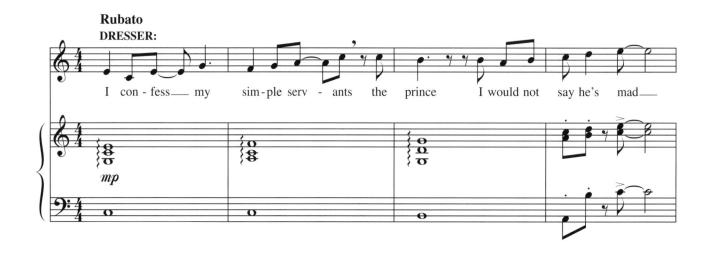

Moderate 4

sim - ple boy sim - ply put he's a sim - ple joy— We're safe and sound— in

his em - ploy 'cause he is a sim - ple boy Some-how he's

sim - ply grown— Sim - ple kind - ness is what he's shown— The kind of prince— we want

on the throne, yes, some-how he's sim - ply grown Al - though I know it

LONDON BRIDGE

Music by NEIL BERG
Lyric by NEIL BERG and BERNIE GARZIA

Moderato

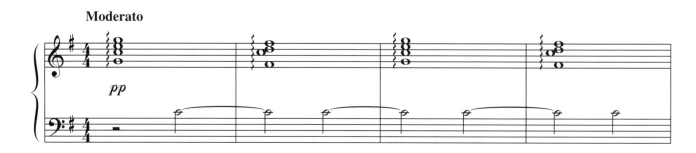

Vamp
PRINCE: *(vocal last time)*

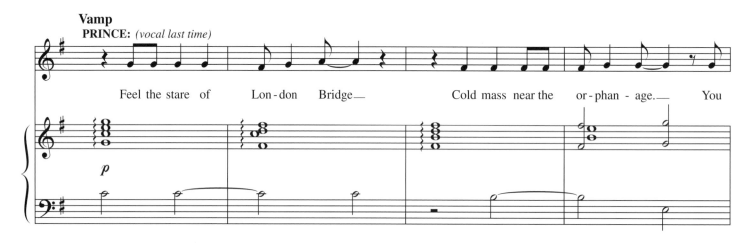

Feel the stare of Lon-don Bridge— Cold mass near the or-phan-age.— You

Colla voce   **Poco rit.**

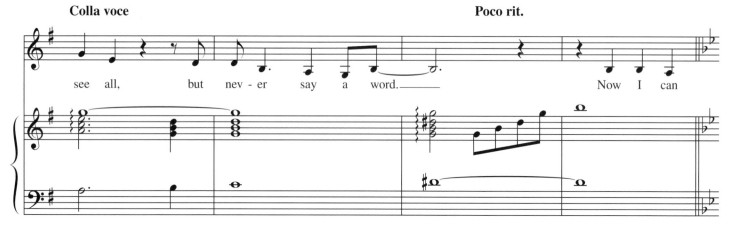

see all, but nev-er say a word.— Now I can

Steady 4

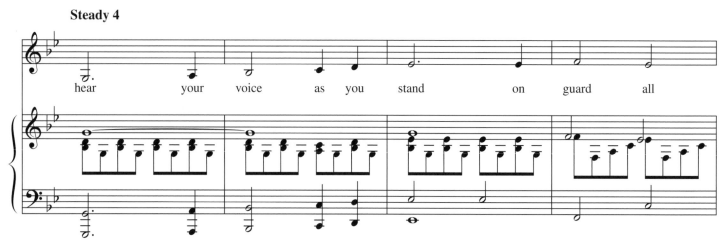

hear your voice as you stand on guard all

Fa - ther,_____ a king you are to them, but should I be a - shamed?

Have I been mis - ta - ken?_____ They

Poco rit.

Più mosso

feel, they bleed, they are lost, they're in des -

Colla voce

Simple (as before)

TWILIGHT

Music by NEIL BERG
Lyric by NEIL BERG and BERNIE GARZIA

Rubato **Colla voce**

MILES:

Sad, this tale of a lone-ly sol-dier who for ten long years, trapped to stay in for-eign cells so far a-way But he pre-vailed, chains un-done He could breathe at last he won his

MY FATHER WAS RIGHT

Music by NEIL BERG
Lyric by NEIL BERG and BERNIE GARZIA

Fa-ther said they're all un-worth-y, the un-washed, ill-bred, un-fed Was he wrong? Now I will see them dead! My fa-ther was

62

right Let them try to take flight   And I'll   cut   each   one   down

with   my   sword!

I could see their   woe and   sad - ness

And I pledged to   ease their pain   Their suf - f'ring   would   not   be   in